1

God created the heavens
and everything in them,
the earth and everything in it.

REVELATION 10:6

Dear God...
You made all things!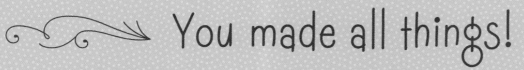

You made the rain, the wind, the snow...

The buds to bloom, the grass to grow.

You made the apples in the tree...

You made the mountains and the sea.

Thank You, God, for making my friend and me.

2

God knows everything.

1 John 3:20

Dear God...
You know all things!

You count the hairs on every head...

You know each thought and what's been said.

You know the size of every tree...

You know the names of all you see.

Thank You, God, for knowing my name.

3

I am the LORD, I do not change.

MALACHI 3:6

Dear God...
You are always just the same!

You are God, the Lord, the Way...

I can trust You when I pray.

When the sky is blue or gray...

You are faithful, come what may!

Thank You, God, for hearing me when I pray.

4

God is love.

1 JOHN 4:8

Dear God...

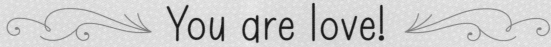 You are love!

Love is patient, kind, and true...

You show love in all You do.

Love can't fail, and love forgives...

Love believes, it hopes, and gives.

Thank You, God, for always loving me.

5

The LORD is good and does what is right.

PSALM 25:8

Dear God...
You are always good!

The Bible says that You are good...

You don't do wrong, You never could.

You are so kind and You are true...

You say good things and do them too.

Thank You, God, for being good to me.

6

The LORD is a great God.

PSALM 95:3

Dear God...

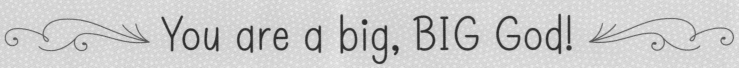 You are a big, BIG God!

You're bigger than the biggest star...

The night-sky shows how GREAT You are.

There's not a thing that You can't do...

You care for me, and help me too!

Thank You, God, for caring for me.

7

LORD, You alone are my cup of blessing.

PSALM 16:5

Dear God...

 You give so much!

You give wonders day and night...
You do what is good and right;
You give peace, and You give joy...
You bless every girl and boy.

Thank You, God, for blessing me.

8

God is everywhere.

JEREMIAH 23:24

Dear God...

You are always here.

Wherever I go You are there...

You are with me everywhere!

When I sleep or when I play...

You are never far away.

Thank You, God, for being with me.

This book belongs to:

_____

It was a gift from:

_____

On:

_____

BIG PRAYERS
for Little Kids

Written by ROY LESSIN and Illustrated by CHRISTI SLATON